remembrances

poems

by

jean lyford

azalea art press

berkeley . california

Azalea Art Press
AzaleaArtPress@gmail.com
http://AzaleaArtPress.blogspot.com

ISBN: 978-0-9849760-9-6

*Dedicated to the memory
of my husband Joe and to my brothers
Lew and Baylis with whom I share
childhood memories.*

CONTENTS

lightness
& darkness

changes
& chances

musings
& imaginings

Foreword:

Jean Lyford has found a new muse these last few years. She has always been a writer—as a journalist, an inspired science teacher, an educator, and even as a humorist in her short stories about her family.

Now she is a poet. All of us who know Jean understand that her poems are her truth, and they thrill and delight us. It is with vicarious joy as well as recognition that we read her poems about her garden and its light, and about her memories and reflections. It is a great boon to all of us, her friends and now her readers, that she found this gift at just the right time.

Jean's first book, *Waves of Time*, created a powerful response in her readers. Her simplicity and clarity supported that connection, and it is even more apparent in this new book of poems. Her poetry, in its lucidity, says simply what we know too in our own observations, allowing us to access our own memories and insights. She is bringing her sense of what we experience to the forefront of our minds.

So is it solace and comradeship that she brings to us? Maybe that, but her poetry also heightens our awareness of the daily mysteries that surround us.

With love and wonderment, we honor Jean's work and courage in publishing these miraculous poems.

- Janet Houck Boreta   *ii*

Preface:

Memories define us. Pain and joy, awareness and forgetfulness all merge into the self we know.

Take away a memory and a lacuna remains that begs for our attention. Poetry allows us to delve into such spaces. Feelings rise to the surface from a past either ignored or forgotten to spur us to absorb more of our life experience.

Sometimes we accept rediscovered pieces of self in small increments; other times seismic shifts in our understanding of the past require us to restructure our life narrative. But once recognized, our memories guide our search for meaning. They remind us who we are.

- Jean Lyford

Memory is the diary
we all carry about with us.

- Oscar Wilde

remembrances

memories

&

reflections

The Breeze

suggests itself

moving branches

bending blossoms

a coolness grazing one's cheek

implying it exists—

like gravity.

Lemon Balm

spreading itself,
blooming in white
with creeping rose geraniums,
scenting a pathway.

Linger in its tartness,
breathe deeply,
hold the scent and
let your breath out in gentle puffs—
it will carry you up the hill
where towhees strut and flutter
between witch-hazel and forsythia.

It's a savory time!
Stay still; notice;
sit on the stone steps;
fondle iris fronds;
let the rosemary's roughness
tickle your nose.
So many scents blend with the wind

and make their own music—

lemon violins, lilac cellos

led by forsythia branches

sweeping, swaying,

keeping time to a rhythm of their own.

Beauty and sadness become one

marrying the past, the present

with an ancient aroma.

Continuum

History's continuum

is a broken graph

with hills to climb

wells without stairs

ropes without pulleys

upside down in space

and lost in time

nevertheless

we do what must be done

to survive a time

to leave a mark

to say

we have travelled here

in time and space

and left something

of ourselves behind

to be recycled.

Daisies

Dancing in the sun
filling the hillside with mirth
waving in a sun-setting breeze
as they tickle my fancy.

A memory of daisy chains,
'he loves me, he loves me not'
while watching bumblebees
stalk pollen
circling blossoms
giving each its due.

Flower heads bend
nodding pleasantries
humming to bees
for seeds to come
following a perfect pattern
dropping into a deep well
the vessel of life.

Alone

but not lonely.
Memories summon up
companionship;
thoughts play with visions
and challenge time.
Old age is not lonely
unless doing is your mantra.
But doing tires feet;
it follows schedules
that may confound
other people's need for regularity.
Alone, but not lonely
gives space to rest or think
or cry or smile or laugh
about the past while
observing the present,
making connections that interweave
into a taut herringbone of time.

Larkspur

A blue mass standing tall
above the fading forget-me-nots
guarding shadows
saving sunlight for themselves.

Sparkle-edged blossoms
swaying in an invisible breeze
engendering motion
dancing in the sun
with a slow bending
of one blossom to another
telling tales,
overlooking alien volunteers
as lesser plants;
they are unaware of legumes
fixing nitrogen
making soil more fertile.

Hummingbirds and butterflies
flutter as they feed
adding to the dance of the breezes,
unifying colors into waves
of delicate blue ripples.

Larkspur, a giant over pansies,
companion to foxglove
lasting longer than both.

The Path

What path have I followed?
Perhaps none.
Perhaps I just meandered
my way from youth
to old age.
Did things just happen
without my noticing?
Were decisions really made
or just discovered?
The winds of change
stole my wandering
blew it into a run
that went on and on—
until I recognized it.

Mustard Field

Golden ripples
dance across the field.
Tall blossoms plié
through the breeze
hovering,
then high kicking
in green tights
lifting cheers
diminishing cares
brightening shadows
under wandering clouds.

Mist

Youth sees clearly

looking ahead,

using the now

as a stepping stone.

Old age sees as if

in a mist,

a fog of memory

that bubbles up

particles from the past,

fragments of being

that have lasted,

melding into a life.

Gardenias

Gardenias waft mists
of memories:
proms and weddings,
shoulders, wrist corsages
as we danced unaware
of youth's beauty,
unknowing of future reveries
when scents bring back
our innocence.

Where Memory Lives

Memory lives where love abides,

where fear falls like shades of night,

where hope rebounds

tested by reality.

Chemicals connect strands,

lock away memories

to fondle later

when hope shortens

in twilight time.

Unlock the safe when hope is gone.

Let yesterday flow,

catching up with time,

adding strength

to a mix of tenses.

Open-handed, open-eyed,

ever-listening:

stir the sauce you've made.

A Kiss

Mouths closed

soft lips together

leaning into one another

eyes shut, noses bent

new feelings

tugging

clasping

nestling

then pulling apart

hands touching

electric surges

on finger tips

smiles

eyes meet

good nights

dreams awakened.

Too soon

pale cheeks

peeling lips

cold forehead

unseeing eyes open

so blue

a blink in memory

give in to time

let the teardrops fall

pull up the sheet—

goodnight

dreamless sleep.

Going Home

Childhood games;
friends next door
where games begin
and spread out into streets
where pick-up games
mix many ages,
boys and girls together
playing softball
hitting windows
or breaking milk-bottles
or falling while
tripping at second base—
the sewer drain.

In late Fall a game of
roller skating hockey
pushing around sycamore balls
woody and full
until down-the-drain means a goal

perhaps even a win.

Giant Steps, Kick-the Can

played after supper

before lightning bugs were

claimed and bottled

as bats appeared and

chased our hair, or so we thought.

Our parents played Bridge

on screened porches

drinking ginger-ale or Hires root-beer

along with malted milk balls or

chocolate-covered raisins.

Sometimes they'd forget about us and

we could stay past bedtime and

tell one another stories or

when older play Spin-the-Bottle.

Going home

to a place no longer there.

Memory

The film of memory
speeds past time.
Its veil covers
like a quilt
protecting old sighs
from reawakening,
offering an old vision
while building a new truth,
reordering the past.

l i g h t n e s s
&
d a r k n e s s

Sunbeam

A Stonehenge sunbeam
pierces the pines and live oaks,
laser-like,
through brush
behind trunks and
low-lying branches
reaching laurel leaves,
raining golden drops
that sparkle
in an oblique ray
traveling across the hillside,
delineating its contour
on a winter's afternoon,
a narrow fiery pendulum
tolling the time of day.

Dark Days

I was born during the dark days
when light leaves early and
returns late;
when we light candles
and trees and
build fires
deep and high
and place shiny things
on the mantel
to reflect what light there is.

A sad time, but
the light we build
and angle and place just so
makes merry with the dark outside.
Stay inside.
Watch the candles flicker.

Study fiery shapes as you
sip a warm drink
and remember other dim days.

Give darkness
a place of its own.

War Time

Shades drawn

dark outside

only the moon

looked down on

men with armbands

air raid captains

seeking light

shown anywhere

to cite and advise us

to pull blackout shades

more carefully

no cracks for light

to escape

and announce

we were there.

Practicing first aid
with pretend tourniquets
and arms in
carefully folded slings
gauze around heads
and shoulders
canes and crutches
in preparation
for bombs.

In daytime
searching skies
looking for airplanes
we had studied
so we could retreat
undercover for enemies
or cheer for our P-38s
that would fight
for us to the death.

We played with soldiers
bought at the five and dime
moving them in the dirt
under a fir tree
in imaginary maneuvers
against the Axis
to win the war.

Gold stars
in some windows
everyone knew what
a knock on the door
might mean
when uniformed men
waited patiently
looking at their feet.

We carefully stripped

the metal lining on the packages

of my father's *Old Gold*

cigarettes—

Lucky Strike Green Has Gone to War

We cleaned tin cans

that we loved to jump on

squashing them into a pile

for the war effort.

We volunteered

as candy stripers

at Bryn Mawr Hospital

or sorted mail at the post office

or planted Victory Gardens.

We saved our pennies to buy

books of stamps that could be

traded in toward a War Bond—

we were patriots.

Parents carefully guarded ration books
for sugar, meat or gas.
Our garden helped meatless Tuesdays.
Sunday drives, nylons, new cars, or radios
would have to wait as did travel—
trains were for troops.
We went to the movies where
a picture of our flag appeared
as we stood and sang
our national anthem.

In addition to double features
we watched short subjects,
cartoons and newsreels
from the North African campaign
against Rommel, the Desert Fox,
who finally lost to the Allies.

The invasion of Italy and D-Day
gave us hope we would
prevail in Europe,
but the horrific losses of
the Battle of the Bulge
and Casino in Italy
where uncles, brothers,
fathers fought and
lost many compatriots
were setbacks.

Despite the hardships,
the worry about our
"boys over there"
the loss of so many,
we felt proud, even exhilarated
as one nation
with a single purpose—
defeat Hitler and Hirohito.

Crystal

Glittering

sparkling

catching light

like fireflies

stroking the air

breathing

puffing a breeze

encircling

a pyramid formed

in the past

bursting forth fireworks

on the hillside

catching light

saving

exploding bits of sun

in facets of glass

before darkness

falls.

Pitch Black

Even in the pitch dark
one can see
if one tries hard enough.
Shapes wave
forming vague outlines
that can be guessed at,
made whole enough
to touch,
to whisper tales of mystery
that dilute black
into paler shades,
gray like the mist,
a gentle fog caressing,
turning blindness
into light,
protecting us from falls
into the abyss
holding us
keeping us

from whatever lies beyond

the pitch black curtain.

Late Night

At Spring Solstice

deep golden

splays across the grass

trips between trees

giving day's death a reprieve

adding depth to shadows

backlighting leaves

in a green glow

giving extra time to play

or view one's garden

in a different light.

I Am Not Here

I'm in another place
full of old demons holding court
building on one another's fears,
dancing with bobbing heads,
arms raised,
fingers splayed
into frozen grasps,
claw-like
in their petrifaction,
never dropping
to touch one another
nor to pick up an instrument.
No accompaniment is required.
The dance goes on from an inner need,
forced as though in a waking dream
when one can push the tale
into a more pleasing place,
but somehow still aware
that another's will guides.

Sleep may dull the fear,

but not the tale.

The story has been lived.

It cannot be changed

nor rearranged in any way.

It abides in memory,

dry and cold,

vague in its reality.

Light is Coming

The light is coming
to fade the dark
and show the world
in tones of grey.
Like washed stones
colors will be clarified, will brighten,
but not yet.
Linger in the faded patterns,
figure out the forms
of trees and paths
that lead to who knows where.
A touch of green
something white
the palest pink
appear as light lifts the shade.
A mystery hangs between
light and darkness,
in the limbo where we live.

On the Edge

I will get on tiptoe

look over the edge

study the blackness beneath

and look so hard

black will turn to grey

then things will become clear

translucent

a vision not above

but below.

Below where many creatures hide

in rivulets or in deeper holes

or even little rills

like a stream of earth

feeding, flowing, flowering

with roots and seeds and

baby things

that live and grow

beneath our feet.

Arise—it's safe up here and
I'm afraid to go below into an abyss.
I'm afraid of depths.
If you come to me I'll greet you
one by one
tale by tale
truth by truth
until I can no longer see you
nor feel you nor hear you.

Darkness parents itself
hugging dimness, crying alone
without stairs to scale upward.
Show yourself; share your truth.
Don't stay buried in my past.
Perhaps I can find a ladder
to help you up from
where you live unknown to me,
where you hide so I can't see you,

where shadows stay in corners

and will not face the day.

A Dry Period

A dry period now.
The lilies are gone; their fronds brown.
Daisies in second bloom
and fading roses bow.
Moisture disappears,
dew escapes, pulled to the sun.

Dry grass
golden
no longer green
with expectation.
Waiting now,
passing from gold
to silvery gray
ready for the
earth to turn.

Dry leaves
rustle in the gutter
blowing their news.

Fall beckons.
A quick step,
a gasp of color
reminds us—
now school begins.

Small World

Small things
gift a garden
filling it with life.

A crimson petal
on the grass;
a chickadee
in the birdbath;
a breeze
turning maples'
sparkling leaves
inside out;
a butterfly circling
then resting on a petunia;
bees and hummingbirds
feeding on lavender;
small creatures of the night
visiting invisibly.

As the world
becomes smaller
one's awareness
grows larger,
deeper.

changes
&
chances

Bleeding is Rain

Bleeding is rain

that may not stop

until the skies have lost their crowns

and tears

no longer run in rivulets

connecting drops of rain

on window panes.

A red river is as salty

as tears;

both echo

the sea that bore us.

Plum Blossoms

Plum blossoms blowing in the wind

pink confetti carrying cares

away from home

swirling in eddies

covering the garden

with pale petals

flying from tree tops

and low branches

like birds leaving the nest

landing on others' lives

easing the burden

of losses

tucked into pockets

waiting for change.

Eyes Open

but unseeing,
not blind,
but willfully so.
It hurts too much.

A pain familiar
rising from the past
unrelenting
until I busied it away
and went off
to other things.

But it's not gone.
It grows slowly
beneath flickering eyelids
and muffed ears.

Is there a time to let it out
to caress troubling scars
ease the raw sting

from long ago,

inhale

shallow breaths

that let the past

linger below?

It's too late

to give up crying.

It's too soon to pack away

what was never opened.

No pain is truly unbearable.

You have been bearing it

all along.

Pine Branches

bent by the wind

in swirls that

harden like an old man's back

pines sway

to a rhythm played

by a silent, invisible orchestra

branches take turns moving

now in unison

then separately

in private embraces

cherishing one another

shaping harmony

until the wind claims them

forcing a fierce note off-key

that breaks branches

extended too far

for too long

succumbing to

the brittleness of old age.

Now I Know What's Beneath

It has been hidden for a long time,

but now it is revealed

if only at night

under cover of darkness,

when others sleep,

it eats into my world

whether I know it or not.

It plays with beams of light

that draw its dancing wings

and let it flutter

in a hectic jitterbug

of retro steps.

Its friends cover the dance floor

with leaps and turns

and spins.

By morning it will be gone,

back to its hideaway.

A few stragglers may

drop in exhaustion

but the dance is over.

What's beneath

will not be seen again

until it decides to dance once more.

Perhaps next Spring.

Knees

not bees'

but mine

pudgy at first

then useful

strong

but flexible

for exercise

for standing

walking

running

tennis

swimming

whatever

until injured

sore and stiff

a shot will help

and did

cycle again

until stairs grow

taller and deeper

and creaks

creep in

not the steps

but my knees

get new ones

of steel or

something else

until

I don't need them

anymore.

Facial Crags

deepen, peel

and crinkle into

crepe with time.

Smiles leave marks

of better days,

a more graceful life

with future dreams untold

but telling

secrets of youth and joy

without understanding

old age.

Turn the mirror

inward;

frame the past;

remember what has been

not what has been lost.

Flatlines

It cannot be good—
flatlines must stay flat.
They do not re-waver
after the sheet is drawn.
When the time comes
I promise to stay still
with eyes unseeing,
weary heart asleep forever.
Do not worry;
I have no exoskeleton
to protect my soft insides.
I will not inveigle a wiggle,
nor turn over to brag
about my existence,
my toughness,
my wiggle-ability.
Only a few tiny creatures
can hold on to their nuclear core
long enough to persevere with

a last gasp beyond the flatline

after the sheet is drawn.

A Garish Garden

makes me smile

at its presumption.

Orange and crimson

blend with

all the gentler shades

into a mix that stirs.

Its playfulness

gives joy to creatures

sharing its shade,

its sustenance, its hiding places.

Poke around.

Wander in and out of paths

that lead to nowhere

but pattern a background

in which to find yourself.

Changes

I'm not as smart as I used to be;

now it's more habit than vision.

Changes confuse and hide things

that used to be at hand.

Why this room?

What is lost?

Where, where, where?

If a gift seems good,

I give it twice

and don't remember.

Changes come slowly as fingers

or thoughts fumble,

tumble out of focus.

Remembering

horses pulling milk wagons

morphs into cardboard cartons

robotically milked

without stool or proverbial maid.

As I get slower, the world

runs ahead of me.

A sense of impatience

as I fiddle producing a credit card

(we used to call them charge plates)

or ask a question or mis-hear an answer

or forget to sign an inkless screen that

doesn't care about my penmanship.

Eye rolls or polite care

belie my abilities.

I do understand a lot even though

I'm not as smart as I used to be.

Faulty Memory

Faulty memory
caresses the past
cuddling pleasure
in a warm embrace
comforting the present
while reshaping pain
excising agony
frozen in cold storage
awaiting retribution
or thawing memory.

Waiting

Waiting for someone

who may not come

wrong time?

wrong place?

wrong date?

was I unclear?

wait just a little longer

think of things to do

lists for the mind

lists I won't remember

things I need

things I don't need

but think I need

just because

they're neat

they're cool

a good idea

that will be recognized

as worthwhile

or

worthwhile

but too expensive

so forget about it

just wait a little longer

he'll walk up and ask

have you been here long?

and I'll pretend

I just got here

even though he'll know I lied

wait just a little longer.

Wondering

mind wandering

fading thoughts

words popping up

then disappearing

only to return

in another form

another format

a lost feeling

inarticulate

but there

below the surface

like the beginning

of something sad

something to come

in another wave

washing over me.

Loss

Each death claims other deaths,

building piles of pain

that overtake,

yet you survive.

Even though the bearing of them

saddens

those losses are true,

they are real,

not an imaginary worry,

nor feeble feelings that fly by,

seeking the light of day

like a lost moth

hiding

then scaling toward the flame.

Our feelings are fine-tuned

to a pitch without harmony,

unable to fly away,

unable to hide;

just feel the tug;

try to move the frozen arm,

try to take in air

and exhale sorrow.

It is real; it is true,

when so much is fleeting.

Hang on to your truth;

examine your pain;

hug it to yourself.

There will be a time

when it is a memory

without stabbing spikes,

without tears,

but rather, a dry memory

until the next loss

brings a reawakening.

Resentment

The river of resentment flows
then stagnates
in a rhythm of its own.
Festering regrets are cleansed
in a fast moving stream
or in a dry season mixed
with putrid algae
jammed upon banks or rocks
rising from a mud bottom.

Time does not cure;
it sorts,
collects blame
and masses misery
into righteous piles.

It clings to injury
and grows until
anger takes its place.

Then the river moves more quickly
washing as it rolls resentment
back into the shadows.

Failure

not success

but failure

enfolds in a thorny embrace

a two-toned rose

its buds sparkling

and stems rough hewn

its wine-tipped edges

circling a golden center

smelling sweet like an old loss

teaching me to cry softly

to catch my breath in one brave gulp

failing, not falling

but learning

learning to find my way

next time

the thorns will be gone

the long stem

will stand tall

and the blossom

will open in a new color.

musings
&
imaginings

A View From Within

This was a year of self-discovery.
In old age one becomes an observer,
of everything—
grandchildren at play,
a cat bounding in the garden,
the curve of hills,
a lone oak guardian,
shadows born of clouds
or the obscurity of fog.
Now there's time to study these things.
Less doing, less coping,
less running in place.

Now even one's self becomes a study,
at first seen from outside,
then discovered from within.
It is not enough to observe.
There is a well, deep and unexplored,
waiting to be recognized

before it's too late to know

how your journey has gone—

why a sense of sadness

or a bubbling up of words

and pictures and sounds

that must be written down

to protect and save

from the failure of memory.

Write.

Let the words rise up

into your throat

and then out

into the air

as you discover

the hidden record

of past feelings

still extant,

still roiling

in the wellspring

waiting to be recognized.

Whispering Leaves

Without wind
or even a breathless breeze
the oak leaves
talk to one another.

Glistening with sunlight
they whisper secrets
saved overnight
impatient
to confide in one another
as the day begins
their communal guarding
of the hillside.

Sometimes tiny bubbles of dew
magnify their glow
exaggerating ripples
of ribald tales they share.

Sometimes they turn away

from light

and show their underbelly,

a paler shade

more vulnerable

as they play together

sharing, but still

keeping secrets,

solemn in their fidelity.

Winter Waiting

Cold earth embraces
incipient corms and bulbs
letting them know it's time to root
and snuggle while nesting in place.

A gentle touch will soon release
them from a crumbling soil.

Spears will force through to test the air
and let the world know
winter wanes.

Another time is coming
green will reach out to
give us hope and confidence.

Life goes on in many tones
to share the budding of a future time.

Be patient—
wait as winter does;

let melting ice and draining water

plump up the soil

into a birthplace

for our dreams.

Heavy Rain

A puddle
unable to find
its way home,
waiting in line
for a turn,
its time,
to pass through
heavy soils,
seeking sand
and space with
air enough,
room enough
to breathe
to purify
to clarify
its purpose.

Black Hole

We have our very own black hole,

invisible, a god-like magnet

centering our galaxy,

its core,

rearranging the universe,

conquering time,

making spirals lose their arms

and crowded clusters move

away from one another.

What happens when the Milky Way

and nearby galaxies

disappear into that abyss?

What spews out from such a stew?

Energy? Light?

Chemicals for new life?

Perhaps, this disappearing act

is the eternal recurrence

of the ancients or

reincarnation—

matter reforming into a mystery,

where blackness and blindness

reshape into

light and vision.

White in the Garden

Even a touch of white defines
the garden's limits,
expanding one's vision beyond—
bold, cheerleading for attention.

In Spring white bursts forth suddenly
and one gasps
at blossomed fruit trees
amassing their tiny points of light.

Pale daffodils, tulips, azaleas
join the chorus
a background
for deep or pastel colors.

When blossoms fade, petals will fall
as gentle wings floating down to rest.
Tiny leaves centered with incipient fruit
will soon emerge to take their place.

Witch-Hazel

Chains of witch-hazel blossoms
cling to the tips of bare branches
like drooping candles yellow as light
announcing life is stirring.

Soon leaf budding will appear
along with forsythia blooms
and pink camellias
that fill the bush with too-perfect shapes
like flowers in a child's book.

Safe Haven

A place beyond the rounded,
blue-grey stones
where boats can rest and oars dry out
where terns and cormorants
dive into calmer seas past the heavy tides
where lobster boats putt-putt across the bay
checking their pots and moving on.

Ducks ignore them
swimming in a row, diving now and then
heads disappear and reappear.
Loons let out a hoot, not quite a laugh,
more like an harrumph.
The back bay moves more slowly
with the sea's ebb and flow,
than at the sea wall where waves crash
and spill over.

The noon sun hits the water
in sharp, sparkled points

as though each light dances

on the edge of a ripple

and the whole bay becomes a sea of

illuminated visitors from another place.

A sailboat glides past the cove

heading for an island

so small only nesting sea birds stop by

to visit a tired pine leaning precariously

unanchored in the sandy soil.

Although small,

the island adds depth to the scene

of Blue Hill Bay across Duck Cove,

beyond far off pines, rooted more securely,

like a deep blue-green fringe of tree tops,

even in a foggy mist, crying out from afar.

On Poetry

Poetry defines itself
a treasured friend
a therapist, safe,
revealing,
insightful.
The unrealized
announces itself
gently with care.

.

Spaces

Spaces have mass

unseen

holding forms

apart from one another

giving surcease

to busy bouquets

or bright lines in a painting

or helping to recognize

lonely trees in the forest.

Patterns

shaped by necessity

culled from chaos

into shapes

we comprehend

carving edges

binding experience

tracing limits

to find patterns

that clarify

our vision.

Write

When you don't know
what you think,
start writing,
even while tears drop
on a blank page.

When you don't know
what to do,
start writing,
even if just a list
of what you could do.

Something will come
from a place you didn't know about,
from a place of silence,
perhaps even a forgotten place
visited in the past.

The scent of lilacs
may bring it back,

or perhaps a child's stray hair

a parent's smile

or just daydreaming.

Something will come

to surprise you,

to teach you,

to remind you

of what has always been there.

What Will It Be Like

to miss shades of green

on witch-hazel leaves

or foxglove eyes in the sunlight

or pansy patterns edging the garden

or the full face of loved ones?

What will it be like?

Will my view be a mirage

of those I once knew

or a haze of daisies

on a pallid hillside?

Will others' feelings

be voiced in nuanced tones

I can understand?

What will it be like?

Will I cry out alone,

or be brave in company?

Will I find a new way

to see ruffles in peonies

or sprays of golden forsythia?

Will I accept such visions?

What will it be like?

Waves Wash Over Me

Waves wash over me,

carry me to a deeper sea

where I float on tender ripples,

buoyant,

breathing in time

to the rhythm of the water.

Misty clouds wander above

following me.

Light sparkles from an unseen source

where the sun hides,

reminding me it still shines

on this bobbing sea

whether troubled or safe

as ebbing waves

pull me

to another, unknown shore.

Acknowledgments

Family support is invaluable for any writer, especially one delving into depths of strong feelings. My children Amy and Joe, spouses Stephanie and Dave, grandchildren Eve and Willa, and brothers Lew and Baylis all remain my touchstone for both strength and love.

Working with Karen Mireau, editor and publisher, is a joy. She prods in such a gentle manner that one discovers afterwards just how much she managed to accomplish in a short time.

My coach, mentor and primary editor, Cynthia Leslie-Bole, saw me through three edits, encouraging all the way. I cannot say enough about the power of classes with Cynthia's coaching in Hummingwords Writing Workshops; sharing with fellow writers and giving positive feedback to one another, we form strong bonds.

Alexandra, Barbara, Catherine, Cindy, Mari, Maureen, and Ruth have heard many of these poems read in the raw before any editing. Thank you, writing friends, for your continuing support.

About the Author

Born and raised in suburban Philadelphia, Jean enjoyed helping her mother in the garden. It is clear from many of her poems that her love for gardening has remained.

Jean received her B.S. from Drexel University, attended

graduate school at Columbia University in literature, and later received an M.A. from St. Mary's College.

Her teaching career began in a Bedford-Stuyvesant junior high school in Brooklyn, New York. After moving to California with her husband and two children, she taught middle school in Orinda for many years. Her husband, Joe, a journalist and writer, died in 1992, the same year she retired.

Writing has always been important to Jean. Arriving at old age has only contributed to her love for poetry and her wonder at the marvels of nature.

Contact:

Jean Lyford

mjlyford@comcast.net

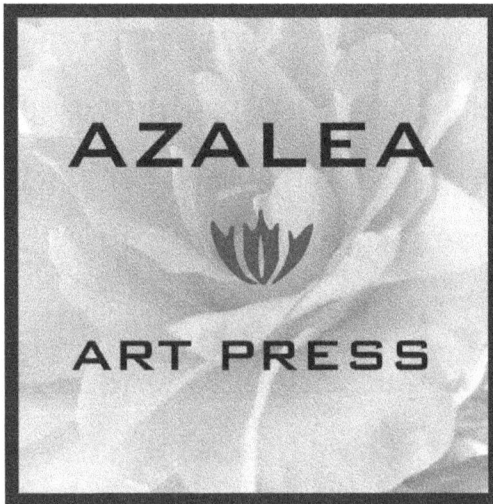

Azalea Art Press

azaleaartpress@gmail.com

www.ingramcontent.com/pod-product-compliance
Lightning Source LLC
Chambersburg PA
CBHW030024290326
41934CB00005B/467